Audio Access Included – *Recorded Accompaniments Online*

AMERICAN ART SONGS
FOR THE PROGRESSING
SOPRANO

ISBN 978-1-4950-8853-7

To access companion recorded piano accompaniments online, visit:
www.halleonard.com/mylibrary

Enter Code
5314-5368-9224-0762

G. SCHIRMER, Inc.

DISTRIBUTED BY

7777 W. BLUEMOUND RD. P.O. BOX 13819 MILWAUKEE, WI 53213

www.musicsalesclassical.com
www.halleonard.com

Pianists on the recordings: [1]Catherine Bringerud, [2]Brendan Fox, [3]Richard Walters, [4]Laura Ward

THE CHILDREN

from *The Children*

Leonard Feeney

Theodore Chanler

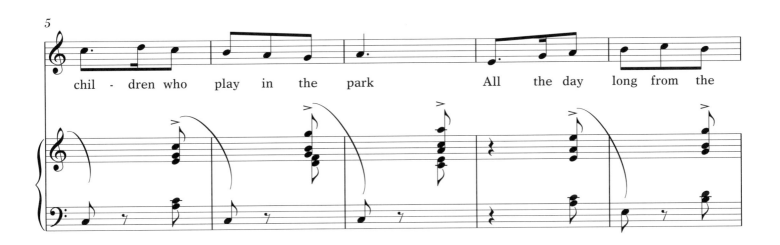

Words used by exclusive permission.

chil - dren? Will there be chil - dren a -

gain, When we who are chil - dren are wo - men and

men? Yes!

Sure - ly the world will love

IT'S ALL I HAVE TO BRING

Emily Dickinson*

Ernst Bacon

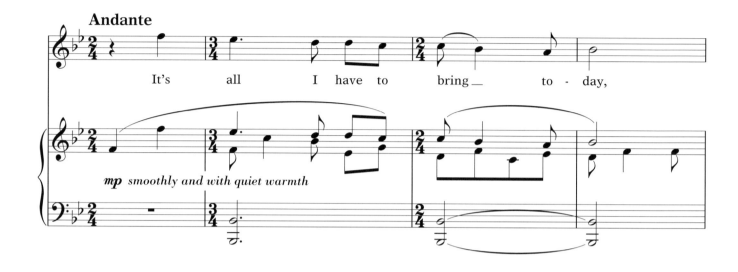

*Words printed by special permission.

LONGING
from *Two Poems of the Wind*

Fiona Macleod (William Sharp)

Samuel Barber

Allegro con grazioso

thee._____ In the dew on the grass is your name, dear, i' the

leaf_____ on the tree—_____ O would I were the

cool wind that's blow-ing from the sea._____ O___

would I were the___ cool___ wind that's__ blow-ing far from___

very softly

Much slower

*The optional note appears in Barber's manuscript.

MOTHER, I CANNOT MIND MY WHEEL

Walter Savage Landor

Samuel Barber

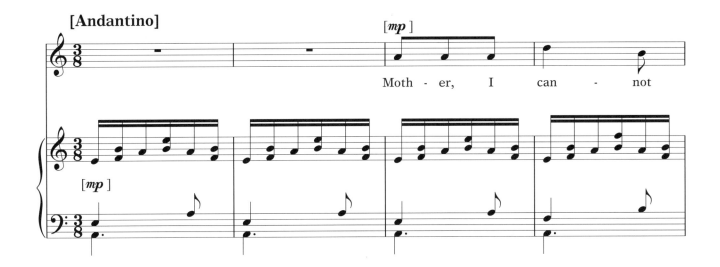

men may use de - ceit;

He al - ways said my eyes were

blue, And of - ten swore my lips were

sweet.

To Daisy
THE DAISIES

James Stephens

Samuel Barber
Op. 2, No. 1

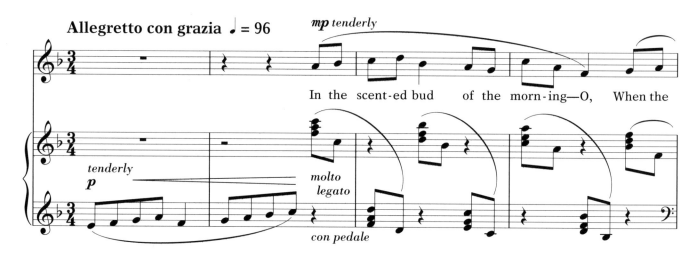

Poem from *Collected Poems of James Stephens.* Printed by permission of The Macmillan Company, publishers.

wan-dered hap - p'ly,★ to and fro; I kissed my dear on ei - ther cheek, In the bud of the morn - ing— O. A lark sang up from the breez - y land, A lark sang down from a cloud a-far, As she and I went hand in hand In the field where the dais - ies are.

★In Stephens' poem the word is "happily," which Barber chose to set on two notes rather than three.

The Windmill,
Rogers Park
July 20, 1927

SOMETIMES I FEEL LIKE A MOTHERLESS CHILD

African-American Spiritual
Arranged by Harry T. Burleigh

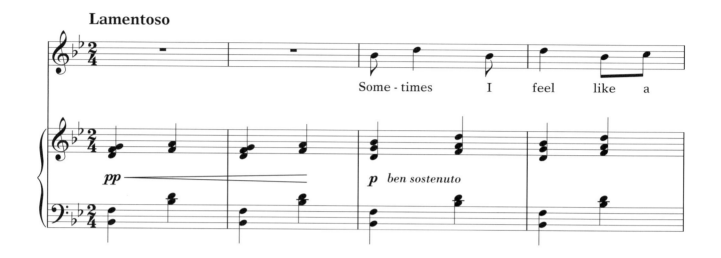

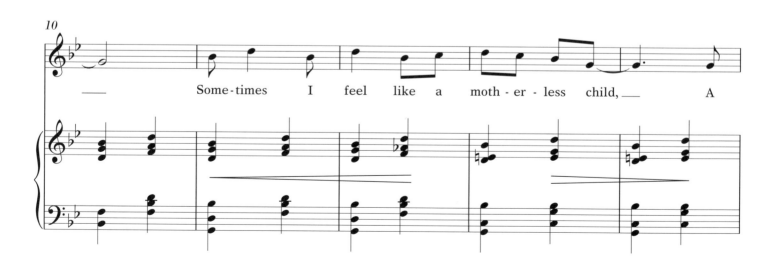

long ways ___ from home, _____ a

long ways ___ from home. _____ A

long ways ___ from home, _____ a

long ways ___ from home. _____

To Lawrence Tibbett

LOVELIEST OF TREES

A. E. Housman*

John Duke

* Poem from "A Shropshire Lad." Printed by permission of Grant Richards, London, publisher.

A - bout the wood - lands I will go To see the cher - ry hung _____ with snow.

for Olive Endres

THE SHEPHERD

William Blake

Lee Hoiby

all __ the day _____ And his tongue shall be

filled _____ with praise. _____

cresc.

For he hears _____ the lamb's in - no - cent call. __

And __ he hears _____ the ewe's

to the Guide
WHERE THE MUSIC COMES FROM

Words and Music by
Lee Hoiby

feel.

I want to
walk in the earth-ly gar - den, Far from cit-ies, far from

fear. I want to talk to the grow-ing gar - den, To the

*pronounced *day – vas* (nature spirits)

THE LASS FROM THE LOW COUNTREE

Text adapted and Music by
John Jacob Niles

To Miriam Witkin

THE GREEN DOG

Words and Music by
Herbert Kingsley

to Helen-Claire Moyle

AMERICAN LULLABY

Gladys Rich

ORPHEUS WITH HIS LUTE

William Shakespeare

William Schuman

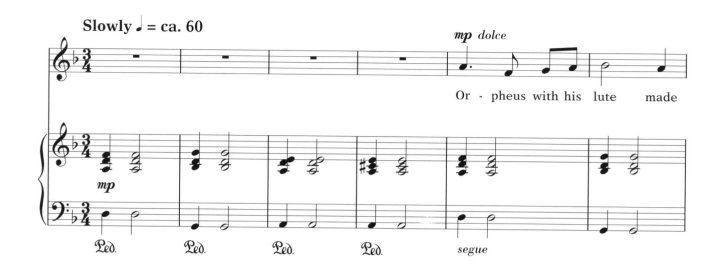

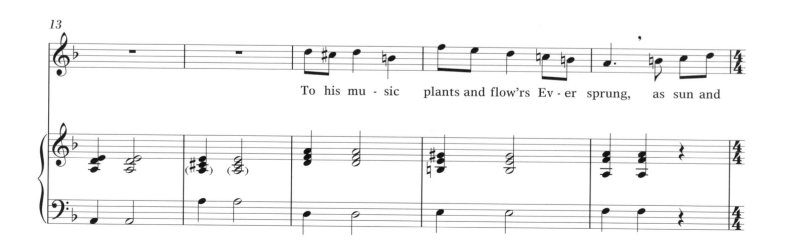

THIS LITTLE ROSE

Emily Dickinson*

William Roy

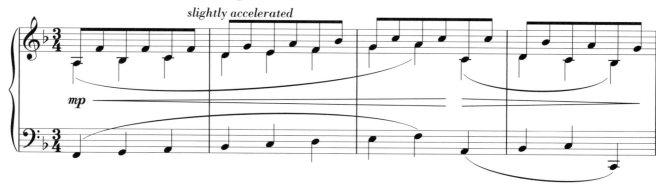

No-bod-y knows this lit-tle rose, It might a pil-grim be.

Did I not take it from the ways And lift it up to thee.

* Poem copyright, 1945, by Millicent Todd Bingham.